Drawing Animals

Written & Illustrated by Belinda Willson

Design & Layout by Jason Willson

FOREWORD

Before commencing any drawing, it is recommended you have at least three different soft pencils, an eraser and a sharpener. 2B, 4B and 6B pencils are preferred and can be purchased from most Art Suppliers and Newsagents.

This book has been designed to encourage the development of good drawing and improve the artist's perception. The studies begin at a relatively easy standard, using a basic four step process to systematically explain the method. The steps are gradually reduced as it is expected the artist will be more aware and techniques, better retained.

As the book progresses, you are encouraged to adopt a more independent approach, thus further enhancing these newly acquired skills.
A series of hints and instructions are included for each illustration.

Good Luck on your path to better drawing!

ISBN: 1 86476 294 2

Axiom Australia
www.axiompublishers.com.au

Printed in Malaysia

PHYSICAL CHARACTERISTICS

Comparative size- 126 Inches: **Elephant.** 63 Inches: **Horse.** 28 Inches: **Lion.** (at shoulders

OBSERVATION DETAILS:

Drawing animals from life is substantially different from drawing humans. Firstly, the illustrator can ask a human to pose, however animals tend to move about making it necessary to initially make fast, and rough sketches. Once this rough is done, fine-tuning can start, adding details as you proceed. Making quick sketches this way assists in heightening your observation skills ensuring more accurate illustration. Obvious things to observe when sketching any animal are size, shape, colour, number of legs, horns, how the animal moves and its outer covering. Once all these details are captured the initial sketch you may then leisurely observe and add muscle tone, skin or fur texture, claw size, shape and any facial expressions.

If life drawing is not for you, there is always illustrating from photographs. This, of course, freezes the action and eliminates the need for hastily drawn roughs, however it may also limit your ability to make fine and accurate observation. Until becoming comfortable sketching from life, this is the next best alternative.

SKELETAL

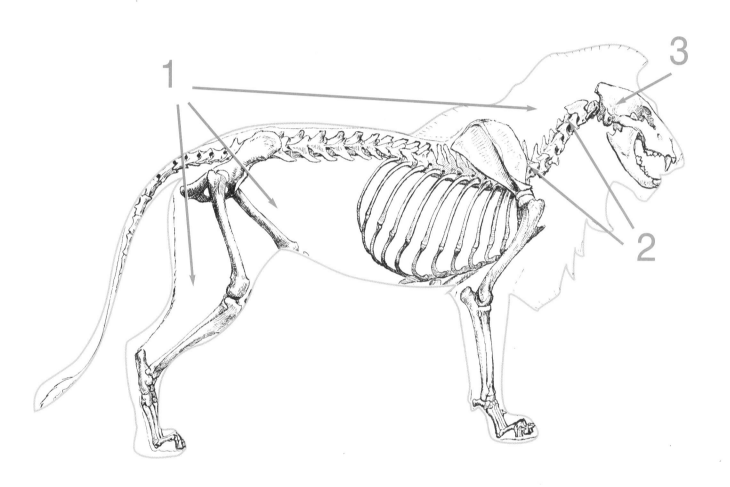

OBSERVATION DETAILS:

1. Notice the bare areas within the body framework. These are largely consumed by muscle tissue supporting and strengthening the skeletal mass.

2. The neck bones of the lion are strong and flexible. They have a unique connection system helping to provide agility needed by the lion in its wide range of head and neck movements.

3. The head is largely bone mass, and almost the entire shape of the head is determined and supported by the skeletal frame.

ANATOMY DRAWING

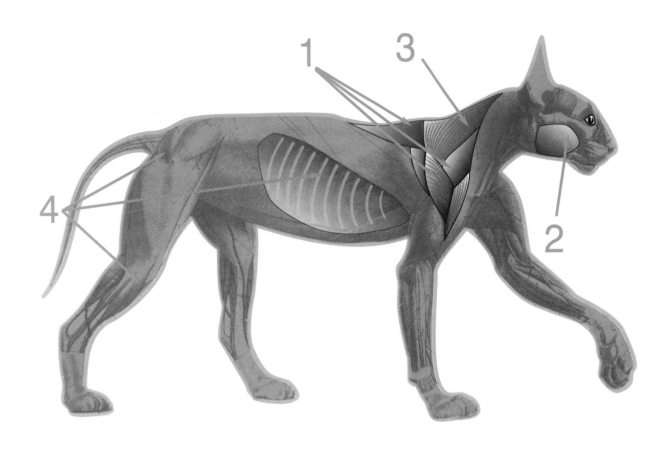

OBSERVATION DETAILS:

This anatomical drawing is from the species of large carnivorous cats including the lion, tiger, and panther.

1. Notice the complex muscle structure within the shoulders and neck areas.

2. As well, the jaw muscles of the cat are rather large and pronounced.

3. The size of the muscular planes are an indication of the strength needed in that area of the anatomy to support the surrounding structure of the body.

4. The cat has sleek body lines with an agile frame and a firm foothold. The ribcage is long and contoured.

PROFILE DRAWING

OBSERVATION DETAILS:

These profiles show in outline form the main step of profile drawing. Once the angle of the profile is set, the detailing of shadows and highlights can be concluded. Obviously there are no angles to this profile, rather a directly side-on view. This being the case the emphasis on the main features will appear as darker shadings. It is therefore suggested that these darker features form the starting point for further shadowed areas. Start here with the main dark areas, progressing to the finer shadow areas and lines. Leaving some clear white areas because they reveal shadows as both deeper and more defined.

AMERICAN TREE FROG

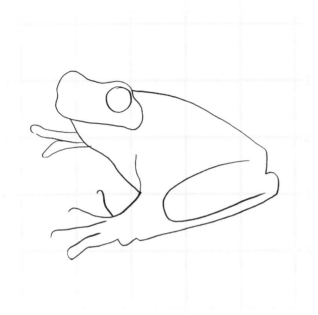

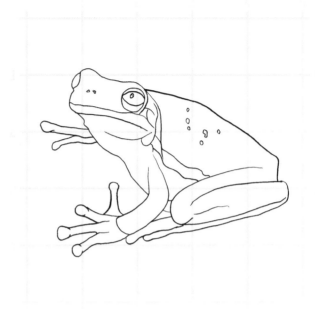

STEP 1:

On your own piece of paper, begin by very lightly drawing a twenty-five square grid using a ruler. A standard 2B pencil is ideal to draw basic circles and lines, as well as the main shapes of the finished sketch. Use the grid to help create accurate proportions.

STEP 2:

Lightly sketching, follow the basic shapes already created and develop the outline of the image and its features. Still focusing on proportions and accuracy.

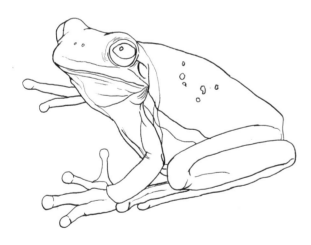

STEP 3:

When satisfied with your outlines, use an eraser to tidy any unnecessary lines or mistakes.

STEP 4:

Using a 4B and 6B pencil to lightly render the image, copy the techniques shown in the example and read the observation details to help achieve an accurate result.

Drawing Animals

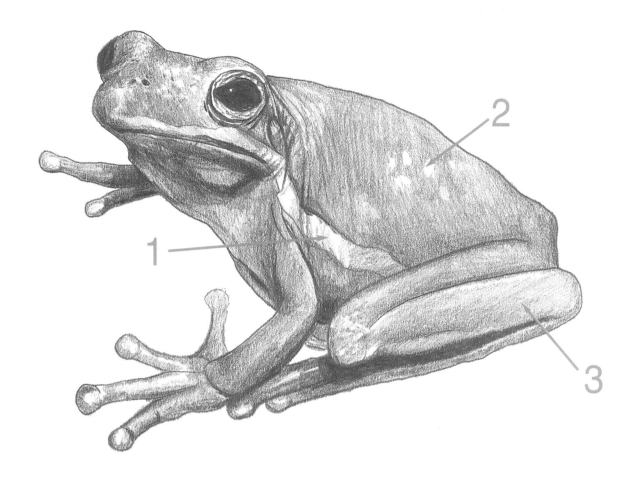

OBSERVATION DETAILS:

1. The stripe along the frog is pale, comparing it with the rest of the body. This area must be rendered in a lighter shade and should be clearly distinguishable.

2. The frog has moisture on its skin, shown by the reflections of light upon its body. In areas of highlight, leave small patches of white to evoke this sense of moisture, contrasting with the texture of the skin.

3. The skin is smooth and should be shaded accordingly. It is recommended you use the side of a 4B pencil, therefore avoiding harsher brush strokes.

KANGAROO

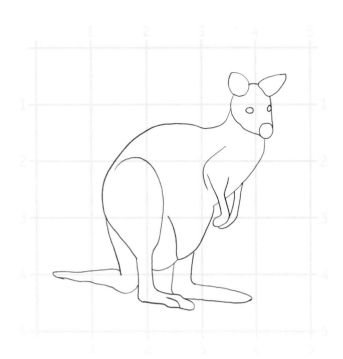

STEP 1:

On your own piece of paper, begin by very lightly drawing a twenty-five square grid using a ruler. A standard 2B pencil is ideal to draw basic circles and lines, as well as the main shapes of the finished sketch. Use the grid to help create accurate proportions.

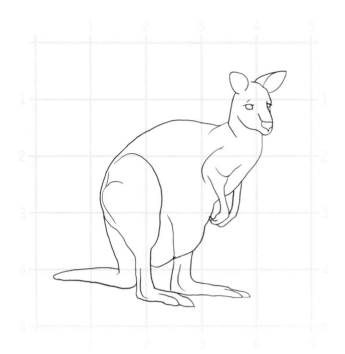

STEP 2:

Lightly sketching, follow the basic shapes already created and develop the outline of the image and its features. Still focusing on proportions and accuracy.

STEP 3:

When satisfied with your outlines, use an eraser to tidy any unnecessary lines or mistakes.

STEP 4:

Using a 4B and 6B pencil to lightly render the image, copy the techniques shown in the example and read the observation details to help achieve an accurate result.

Drawing Animals

OBSERVATION DETAILS:

1. The kangaroo has oversized hind legs and feet when compared to the smaller front arms and paws. Use the length of your pencil to check measurements of these features against your own illustration.

2. The tail is long, very heavy and should be drawn accordingly, noting the tail falls straight down and then trails along the ground.

3. The eye area is quite dark. Although over-rendering this area should be monitored as the eyes and facial features may lose their impact.

4. The eyes are focussed on something in the foreground off to the right, catching the kangaroo's attention. The ears should be turned in the same direction, giving the more alert expression.

ELEPHANT

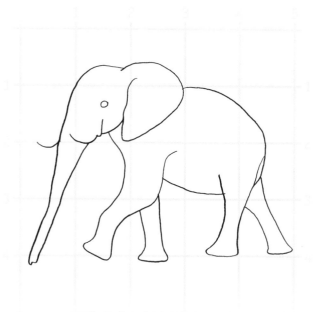

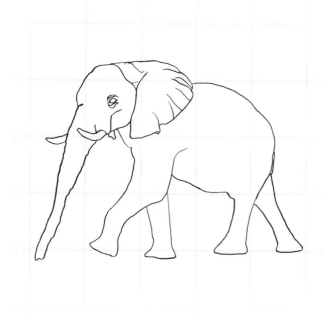

STEP 1:

On your own piece of paper, begin by very lightly drawing a twenty-five square grid using a ruler. A standard 2B pencil is ideal to draw basic circles and lines, as well as the main shapes of the finished sketch. Use the grid to help create accurate proportions.

STEP 2:

Lightly sketching, follow the basic shapes already created and develop the outline of the image and its features. Still focusing on proportions and accuracy.

STEP 3:

When satisfied with your outlines, use an eraser to tidy any unnecessary lines or mistakes.

STEP 4:

Using a 4B and 6B pencil to lightly render the image, copy the techniques shown in the example and read the observation details to help achieve an accurate result.

Drawing Animals

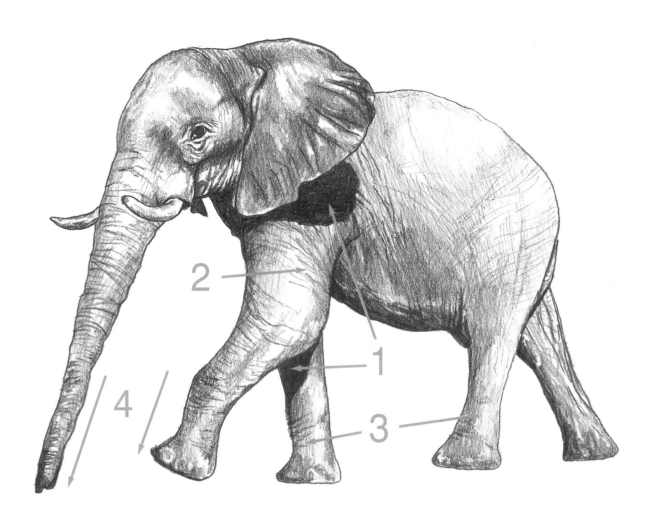

OBSERVATION DETAILS:

1. The darkest parts of this composition are shadows behind the ears and legs. All other sections displaying shadow should be a few tones lighter.

2. The elephant has thick skin with repeated wrinkles upon it. These drawn lightly over the areas of highlight, therefore not dominating the illustration.

3. The elephant's weight is placed on the two legs in the middle of the composition. The other two legs, at the front and rear, should be positioned slightly raised therefore ensuring weight distribution appears in perspective. Also aiding in the expression of movement.

4. The trunk should be drawn at the correct length and parallel to the raised front leg.

BLACK RHINOCEROS

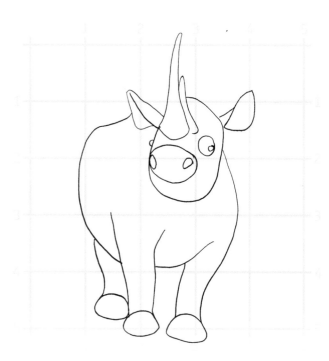

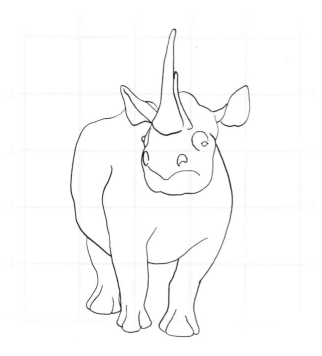

STEP 1:

On your own piece of paper, begin by very lightly drawing a twenty-five square grid using a ruler. A standard 2B pencil is ideal to draw basic circles and lines, as well as the main shapes of the finished sketch. Use the grid to help create accurate proportions.

STEP 2:

Lightly sketching, follow the basic shapes already created and develop the outline of the image and its features. Still focusing on proportions and accuracy.

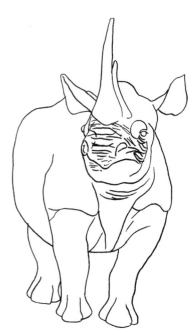

STEP 3:

When satisfied with your outlines, use an eraser to tidy any unnecessary lines or mistakes.

STEP 4:

Using a 4B and 6B pencil to lightly render the image, copy the techniques shown in the example and read the observation details to help achieve an accurate result.

Drawing Animals

OBSERVATION DETAILS:

1. The rhinoceros is substantially wrinkled on the majority of skin. This effect should be drawn lightly over the top of your rendering, naturally without dominating.

2. The Rhino is looking toward the left of the page. The eyes and head should follow this gaze.

3. The horns on his head and the pointed lip are particular characteristics of the Black Rhinoceros and need to be copied accurately.

4. The Rhino's toes are spread across the ground, creating a firm foundation for supporting the heavy body. The way in which the toes angle outwards indicate the strength of this animal.

Drawing Animals

AMERICAN BISON

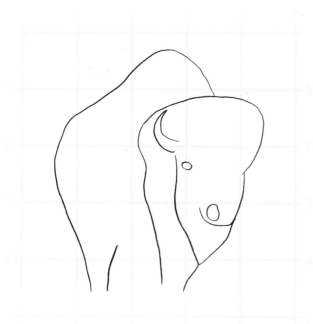

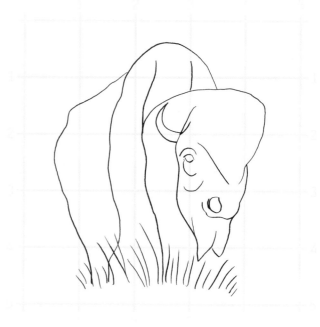

STEP 1:

On your own piece of paper, begin by very lightly drawing a twenty-five square grid using a ruler. A standard 2B pencil is ideal to draw basic circles and lines, as well as the main shapes of the finished sketch. Use the grid to help create accurate proportions.

STEP 2:

Lightly sketching, follow the basic shapes already created and develop the outline of the image and its features. Still focusing on proportions and accuracy.

STEP 3:

When satisfied with your outlines, use an eraser to tidy any unnecessary lines or mistakes.

STEP 4:

Using a 4B and 6B pencil to lightly render the image, copy the techniques shown in the example and read the observation details to help achieve an accurate result.

Drawing Animals

OBSERVATION DETAILS:

1. The bison has long shaggy hair over its entire body. Using regular pencil strokes, make the hair as realistic as possible. Being aware of the varying lengths as in some cases they may appear as tufts.

2. Large areas of the body are dark. Therefore light upon the body is very important when illustrating different sections of both body and facial features.

3. As the bison's hooves are hidden under long hair, to increase the visual interest of the composition add grass at the base of the animal. This creates a platform and a setting for the bison, perhaps giving the early stages for a more expansive illustration showing further environment.

POLAR BEAR

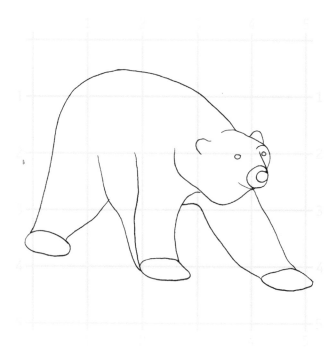

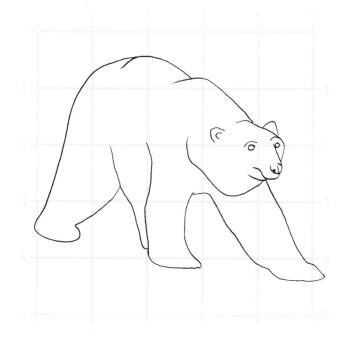

STEP 1:

On your own piece of paper, begin by very lightly drawing a twenty-five square grid using a ruler. A standard 2B pencil is ideal to draw basic circles and lines, as well as the main shapes of the finished sketch. Use the grid to help create accurate proportions.

STEP 2:

Lightly sketching, follow the basic shapes already created and develop the outline of the image and its features. Still focusing on proportions and accuracy.

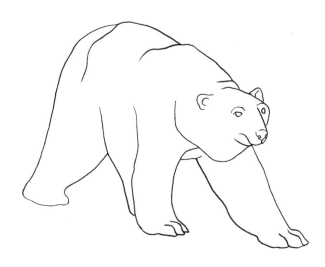

STEP 3:

When satisfied with your outlines, use an eraser to tidy any unnecessary lines or mistakes.

STEP 4:

Using a 4B and 6B pencil to lightly render the image, copy the techniques shown in the example and read the observation details to help achieve an accurate result.

Drawing Animals

OBSERVATION DETAILS:

1. In this composition, the polar bear's hind leg is hidden behind the front. Without letting this hidden leg blend into the front one as the effect can become visually confusing. It is recommended you render the hind leg darker than the front.

2. The shape of the polar bear's head is distinctly different to other bears. Attention should be paid where the eyes and ears fall in relation to all other features.

3. The polar bear's body is extensively shadowed due to the direction of the light source. Unwarrented heavy shading reduces body curves and creases, becoming almost impossible without emphasis on muscle tonings.

Drawing Animals

KOALA

STEP 1:

On your own piece of paper, begin by very lightly drawing a twenty-five square grid using a ruler. A standard 2B pencil is ideal to draw basic circles and lines, as well as the main shapes of the finished sketch. Use the grid to help create accurate proportions.

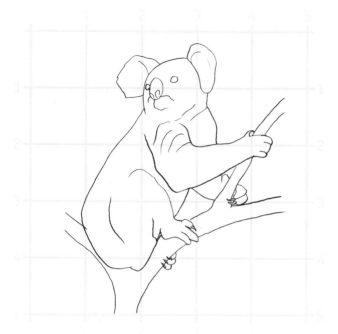

STEP 2:

Lightly sketching, follow the basic shapes already created and develop the outline of the image and its features. Still focusing on proportions and accuracy.

STEP 3:

When satisfied with your outlines, use an eraser to tidy any unnecessary lines or mistakes.

STEP 4:

Using a 4B and 6B pencil to lightly render the image, copy the techniques shown in the example and read the observation details to help achieve an accurate result.

Drawing Animals

OBSERVATION DETAILS:

1. The ears of the koala are very fluffy and quite round. Pencil strokes should reflect this, especially along the edges. Flicking gently only with the pencil to create this effect, because pressing too firmly is not recommended. Perhaps practise on a separate piece of paper until the style is perfected.

2. The fur falls into layers especially along the arms and shoulders and these patterns should be varied in their intensity. Locating thicker lines which form the creases of the body, these will be darker and are most important, controlling the form of the koala and making the pose more realistic.

3. The koala's bottom follows the line of the tree. Consequently there should not be a gap between the koala and the branch. The bottom of the koala is fluffy and soft and melds into the crook of the tree.

HARP SEAL

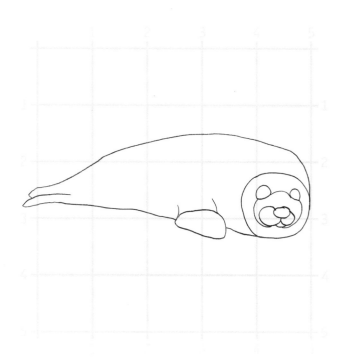

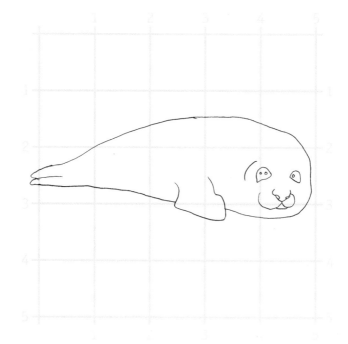

STEP 1:

On your own piece of paper, begin by very lightly drawing a twenty-five square grid using a ruler. A standard 2B pencil is ideal to draw basic circles and lines, as well as the main shapes of the finished sketch. Use the grid to help create accurate proportions.

STEP 2:

Lightly sketching, follow the basic shapes already created and develop the outline of the image and its features. Still focusing on proportions and accuracy.

STEP 3:

When satisfied with your outlines, use an eraser to tidy any unnecessary lines or mistakes.

STEP 4:

Using a 4B and 6B pencil to lightly render the image, copy the techniques shown in the example and read the observation details to help achieve an accurate result.

Drawing Animals

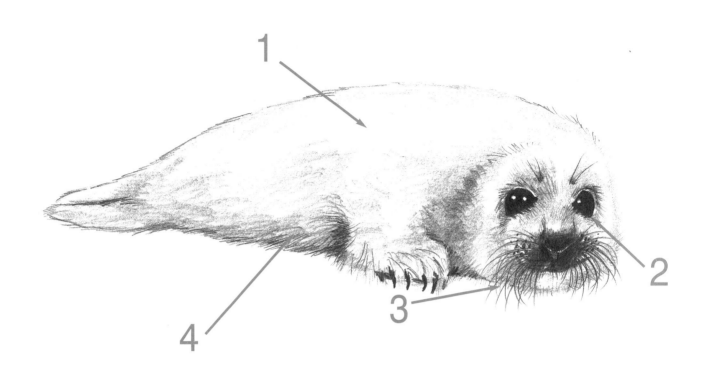

OBSERVATION DETAILS:

1. The majority of the young seal's coat is white. Therefore a careful study of shaded areas will be emphasised with lightly shaded areas only. Leave the highlighted sections along the top of the body without any shading.

2. The seal's eyes are black and require the use of a 6B pencil. Reflections are vital giving them life, mark where they will fall and shade around them.

3. Whiskers should be sharp and precisely drawn. Sharpen your pencil to a point, then make strong even strokes in a downward curve. Vary the strokes enabling some to overlap others, but not too heavily. Then to create the tapered ends, gently flick the pencil.

4. Edges of the seal's fur needs to give the feeling of fluffiness and density. Drawing along these edges in soft strokes, follow the direction of the coat. Keep it fainter near the head where very careful shading is more important.

Drawing Animals

RINGTAIL POSSUM

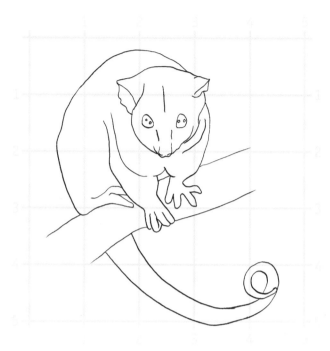

STEP 1:

On your own piece of paper, begin by very lightly drawing a twenty-five square grid using a ruler. A standard 2B pencil is ideal to draw basic circles and lines, as well as the main shapes of the finished sketch. Use the grid to help create accurate proportions.

STEP 2:

Lightly sketching, follow the basic shapes already created and develop the outline of the image and its features. Still focusing on proportions and accuracy.

STEP 3:

When satisfied with your outlines, use an eraser to tidy any unnecessary lines or mistakes.

STEP 4:

Using a 4B and 6B pencil to lightly render the image, copy the techniques shown in the example and read the observation details to help achieve an accurate result.

Drawing Animals

OBSERVATION DETAILS:

1. The branch the possum is holding on to can be left in line only. Contrasting with the heavy shading of the possum's body and making the animal more outstanding as an art piece.

2. The tail curving at the bottom should be left white, consistent with the marsupials' common markings. Apply a little shading to the shadows, giving dimension, especially where the tail curls.

3. The fur is quite fluffy and dark. Use the side of your 6B pencil, shading lightly at first, then building texture as necessary.

DEER

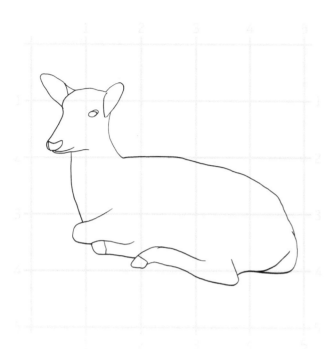

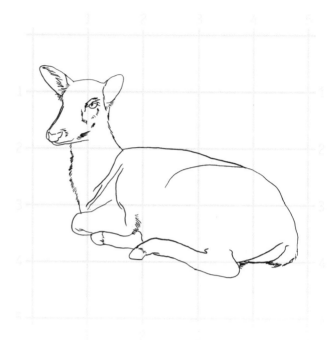

STEP 1:

On your own piece of paper, begin by very lightly drawing a twenty-five square grid using a ruler. A standard 2B pencil is ideal to draw basic circles and lines, as well as the main shapes of the finished sketch. Use the grid to help create accurate proportions.

STEP 2:

When satisfied with this outline stage, erase unnecessary lines or mistakes so that your illustration is both neat and well-proportioned.

STEP 3:

Use a 4B and a 6B pencil to lightly render the deer. Copy the techniques shown in the example and read the observation details to help achieve an accurate result.

Drawing Animals

OBSERVATION DETAILS:

1. The spots on the deer's body are not rendered, but instead are left to show the whiteness of the paper background. Avoid outlining these spots before shading their surrounds. Create as you proceed by carefully examining the above illustration. This will finish as a more realistic effect of fur.

2. Note the way in which the deer has muscles and bones protruding from the bulk of the body when in a laying position. These details ensure more accurate perspective and composition, keeping the body in proportion and alertness.

3. Similarly to that of the kangaroo, the ears and eyes should be drawn alert and facing a particular spot, therefore increasing the keen expression.

4. The main focal point for this illustration is the head, together with its spots along the top of its body. The stomach region, legs and tail can be rendered with minimal coverage.

CHIMPANZEE

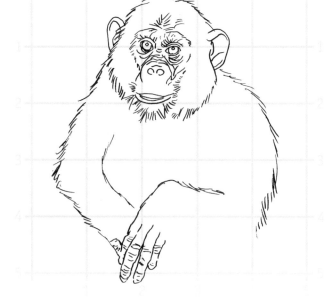

STEP 1:

On your own piece of paper, begin by very lightly drawing a twenty-five square grid using a ruler. A standard 2B pencil is ideal to draw basic circles and lines, as well as the main shapes of the finished sketch. Use the grid to help create accurate proportions.

STEP 2:

When satisfied with this outline stage, erase unnecessary lines or mistakes so that your illustration is both neat and well-proportioned.

STEP 3:

Use a 4B and a 6B pencil to lightly render the chimpanzee. Copy the techniques shown in the example and read the observation details to help achieve an accurate result.

Drawing Animals

OBSERVATION DETAILS:

1. The fur on the chimp's body can be drawn in a sketchy manner, varying the pencil strokes and making it appear to move in different directions. At the same time altering the length will ensure a more realistic feature.

2. The chimp's pose in this illustration does not require including the rest of the body. Compositions such as this are enhanced by features represented which would normally be lost if the entire animal was drawn. Both hands and the facial expressions alter the mood and tell more about character and emotion.

3. As most of the chimp's body hair is black, areas of highlight become very important. Equally the arms are significant to the composition as they have areas of white showing through to contrast the darkness of the head.

4. Take care not to shade the face too heavily as the eyes and nose areas once again reveal personality and emotions, a most significant attraction when drawing with a creature having such creative characteristics.

JAGUAR

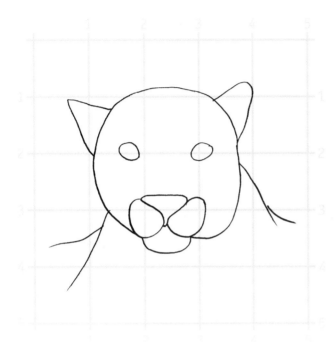

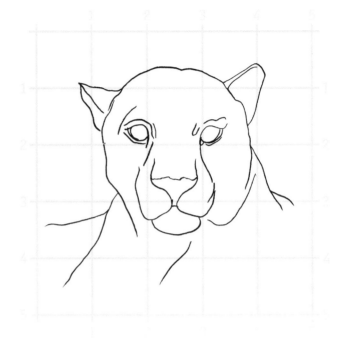

STEP 1:

On your own piece of paper, begin by very lightly drawing a twenty-five square grid using a ruler. A standard 2B pencil is ideal to draw basic circles and lines, as well as the main shapes of the finished sketch. Use the grid to help create accurate proportions.

STEP 2:

When satisfied with this outline stage, erase unnecessary lines or mistakes so that your illustration is both neat and well-proportioned.

STEP 3:

Use a 4B and a 6B pencil to lightly render the jaguar. Copy the techniques shown in the example and read the observation details to help achieve an accurate result.

Drawing Animals

OBSERVATION DETAILS:

1. Spots on the jaguar's coat are irregular and each takes a different form. Avoid using similar patterns, tempting as it might be. Rendering needs to follow the form of the head as it curves. Equally the direction of the fur must be observed to help add dimension to your drawing.

2. The eyes are important as they should stare directly at the viewer. The jaguar is a hunter and this pose is typical, showing a feeling of confidence and power. Placement of the reflections is important. If executed incorrectly, they can make the animal's eyes appear cross-eyed or disproportionate.

3. The jaguar's throat and chest can be drawn in a sketchy style and should fade, adding edges to give a well-balanced composition, whilst concentrating the viewer's attention to the face.

HIPPOPOTAMUS

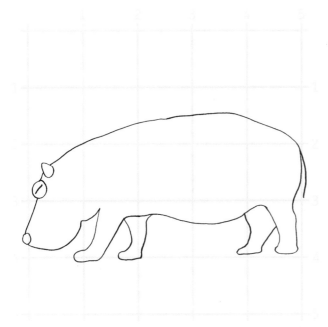

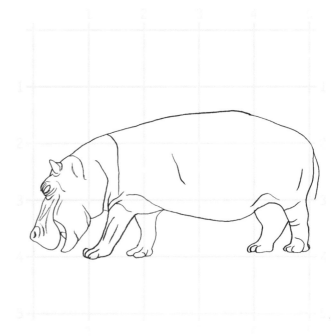

STEP 1:

On your own piece of paper, begin by very lightly drawing a twenty-five square grid using a ruler. A standard 2B pencil is ideal to draw basic circles and lines, as well as the main shapes of the finished sketch. Use the grid to help create accurate proportions.

STEP 2:

When satisfied with this outline stage, erase unnecessary lines or mistakes so that your illustration is both neat and well-proportioned.

STEP 3:

Use a 4B and a 6B pencil to lightly render the hippopotamus. Copy the techniques shown in the example and read the observation details to help achieve an accurate result.

Drawing Animals

3

2

1

OBSERVATION DETAILS:

1. The shading below the hippo should be softer than the rendering used for the body. It is a shadow and should not dominate the picture or blend in with feet.

2. The muzzle has protruding hairs and is quite dimpled. The shaded areas around the muzzle should be rendered in small sections, increasing the feeling of texture, with small hairs drawn after shading is completed.

3. The shape of the hippo's head is rather solid with little variation in definition or form. Therefore the eyes, nostrils and ears become features of interest within the composition. These should be conspicuous and not be lost in shading.

LIONESS

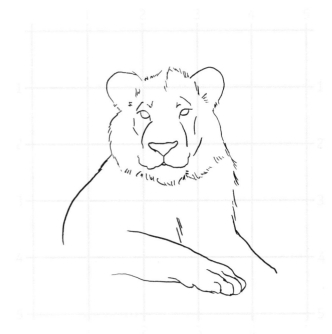

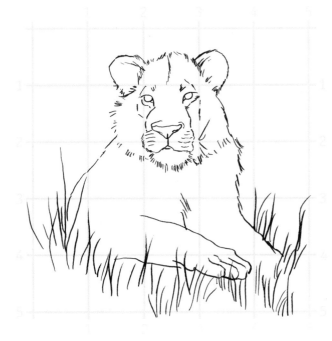

STEP 1:

On your own piece of paper, begin by very lightly drawing a twenty-five square grid using a ruler. A standard 2B pencil is ideal to draw basic circles and lines, as well as the main shapes of the finished sketch. Use the grid to help create accurate proportions.

STEP 2:

When satisfied with this outline stage, erase unnecessary lines or mistakes so that your illustration is both neat and well-proportioned.

STEP 3:

Use a 4B and a 6B pencil to lightly render the lioness. Copy the techniques shown in the example and read the observation details to help achieve an accurate result.

Drawing Animals

OBSERVATION DETAILS:

1. The white fur immediately under the eyes should not be rendered. This area encourages the viewer to the intense expression of the lioness' eyes. Eyes should be clear and rendered only slightly around the edges.

2. The paws become a mere suggestion as to the pose of the lioness. Only slight rendering is necessary in front of the animal because foliage is shown. This encourages the viewer to focus directly on the important facial area.

3. The fur around the eyes needs to be softly rendered, with only the shadows being heavier. This will allow the muzzle to be more a feature and appear dimensional.

4. When drawing the grass, extend the strokes below the leg of the lioness. The grass should also be drawn in sections with pencil strokes taking different directions, giving a more realistic effect.

GIRAFFE

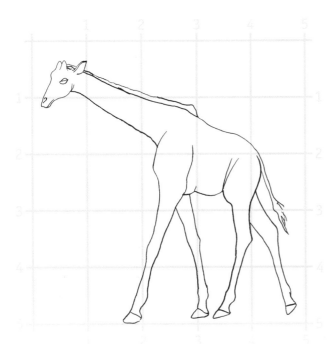

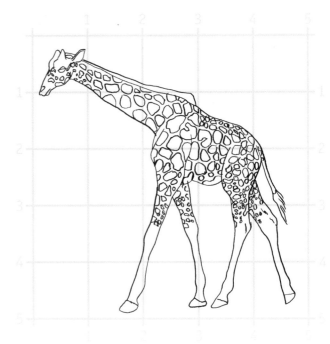

STEP 1:

On your own piece of paper, begin by very lightly drawing a twenty-five square grid using a ruler. A standard 2B pencil is ideal to draw basic circles and lines, as well as the main shapes of the finished sketch. Use the grid to help create accurate proportions.

STEP 2:

When satisfied with this outline stage, erase unnecessary lines or mistakes so that your illustration is both neat and well-proportioned.

STEP 3:

Use a 4B and a 6B pencil to lightly render the giraffe. Copy the techniques shown in the example and read the observation details to help achieve an accurate result.

Drawing Animals

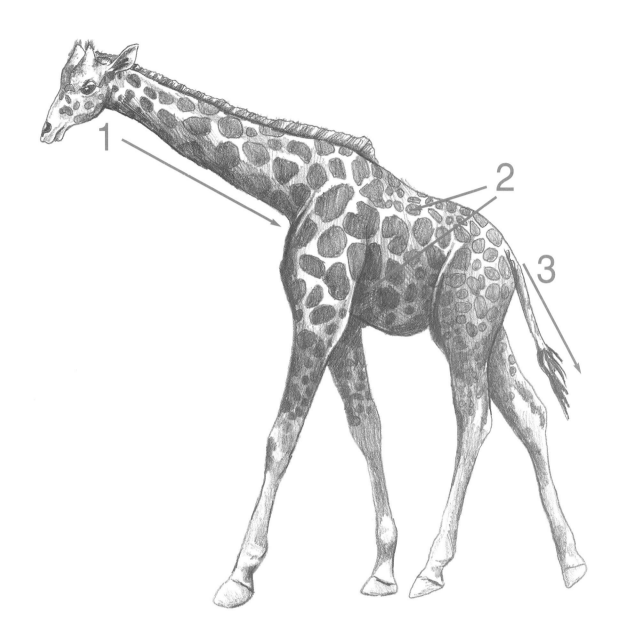

OBSERVATION DETAILS:

1. The giraffe has a long slender neck extending from the centre of the body and far in front of the legs. This extension should be measured by using a pencil as a ruler. The neck, drawn the wrong length will seem out of proportion.

2. The characteristic patterns along the giraffe's body should be rendered before any other areas are addressed, such as shadows. The patches along the top of the giraffe and its rump should be shaded lightly, whereas the patches around the belly are darker.

3. The tail should be an extension of the giraffes neck and spine, and drawn at the same time as the first two features. The tail length is important and once again can alter the proportion of the giraffe by being too long or short.

BEAVER

STEP 1:

Use a 2B pencil to draw the outline and details of the image. Follow the example by creating the main features, as depicted within the finished sketch. When this stage is reached you may need to erase any unnecessary lines or mistakes.

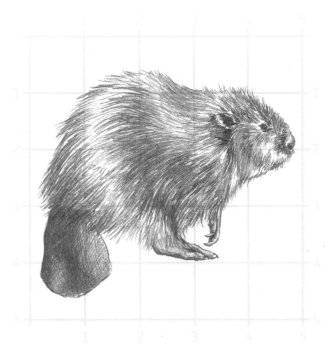

STEP 2:

Using a 4B and a 6B pencil to lightly render the image, copy the techniques shown in the example and read the observation details to help achieve an accurate result.

Drawing Animals

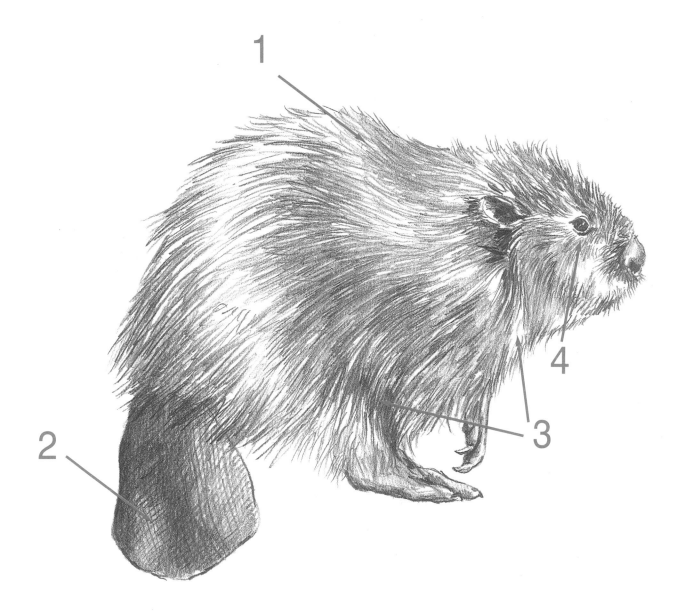

OBSERVATION DETAILS:

1. The beaver has a strange shaped body. By carefully examining this, it will enable all features to be placed in proportion.

2. The textured pattern on the surface of the tail helps develop form. The lines show the way in which the tail curves and gives more dimension.

3. The beaver is a great swimmer, with hair being quite streamlined. The direction in which you execute your hair strokes is very important. Keeping the strokes light and only darkened when the fur is in areas of shadow.

4. The eyes are rather small, comparing these to the bulk of the head and body. The eye being an important aspect should not be lost amongst the hair strokes. Again the eye should be rendered a few tones darker than that of the fur.

GORILLA

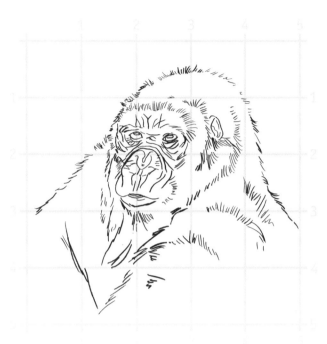

STEP 1:

Use a 2B pencil to draw the outline and details of the image. Follow the example by creating the main features, as depicted within the finished sketch. When this stage is reached you may need to erase any unnecessary lines or mistakes.

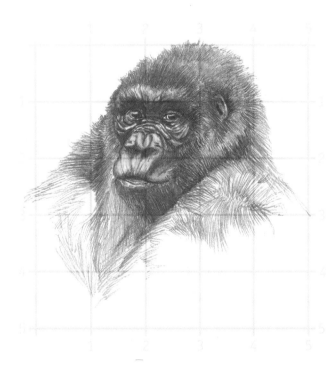

STEP 2:

Using a 4B and a 6B pencil to lightly render the image, copy the techniques shown in the example and read the observation details to help achieve an accurate result.

Drawing Animals

OBSERVATION DETAILS:

1. The gorilla has naturally black hair and drawing this can pose a problem if over-rendering occurs, especially in the face. Drawing the facial features first, slowly render by building in layers. Avoid the temptation of rendering areas which should show as white.

2. When finding you have rendered over a small area, which should be white, use the edge of your eraser to gently lift the pencil impressions.

3. The hair along the gorilla is textured and drawn using the tip of a sharp pencil rather than the side.

4. When drawing a picture with extensive shading, avoid smudging with your hand. Take a separate clean piece of paper and place it where your hand is resting. This minimises smudges and keeps the hand free from graphite.

WOLF

STEP 1:

Use a 2B pencil to draw the outline and details of the image. Follow the example by creating the main features, as depicted within the finished sketch. When this stage is reached you may need to erase any unnecessary lines or mistakes.

STEP 2:

Using a 4B and a 6B pencil to lightly render the image, copy the techniques shown in the example and read the observation details to help achieve an accurate result.

Drawing Animals

OBSERVATION DETAILS:

1. The fur on the wolf's body is very thick and can be represented correctly by keeping pencil strokes irregular and in sections, forming patterns along the creases of the neck where the fur is thickest, then smoother further down the body.

2. The rear of the wolf is drawn in line, contrasting the busy nature of the rendering closer to the the head. The lines can trail off but still follow the form of the body.

3. To make the hair seem realistic, the strokes of the pencil should flick up at the ends and follow the folds of skin and direction in which the hair is flowing.

4. Due to darker shading around the eyes, the eyeball is almost untouched, making it conspicuous, thereby becoming a feature.

SEA OTTER

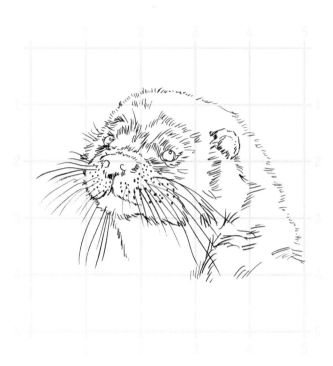

STEP 1:

Use a 2B pencil to draw the outline and details of the image. Follow the example by creating the main features, as depicted within the finished sketch. When this stage is reached you may need to erase any unnecessary lines or mistakes.

STEP 2:

Using a 4B and a 6B pencil to lightly render the image, copy the techniques shown in the example and read the observation details to help achieve an accurate result.

Drawing Animals

OBSERVATION DETAILS:

1. The facial features of the otter need to be strongly noted and emphasised from the rest of the fur on the head. Only areas of shadow should be shaded, leaving the rest of the fur purely as strokes in line with the contours of the body.

2. The muzzle has obvious dimples, which should not dominate the area but instead complement it and blend in with shadows underneath.

3. The eyes, nose and centre of the ears should be the darkest regions of the drawing and for best results created using a 6B pencil.

4. The otter's body is covered in fur, so illustrating as a hard line is incorrect.

RABBIT

STEP 1:

Throughout this book, you have learnt to visualise, capture proportions and render accurately your image. Once drawing with confidence, focus on this image and then try to recreate using all the techniques mastered.

Drawing Animals

OBSERVATION DETAILS:

1. In contrast to the beaver, the rabbit has very soft, fluffy fur. Using the side of your pencil, lightly render the fur. It should appear smooth along the top of the rabbit's back and rougher for chest hair.

2. The leaves at the base of the illustration give the rabbit a setting in which it is existing, instead of appearing to float in mid-air.

3. The rabbit has long eyelashes and whiskers. Use a sharp pencil very lightly flicking the end to taper out the lines, after the rest of the picture has been shaded.

4. The ears, turning in two different directions show the rabbit as alert to its surroundings. The eyes, focused forward, with each ear facing the opposite direction. These subtle details bring the rabbit to life and therefore true to its nature.

ANIMAL DESCRIPTIONS

To best capture the essence and character of your subject, as well as develop as an artist, a study and understanding of your choice of subject is most important. Here is a short description of the animals included in this book. These are brief explanations only and it is recommended that a more extensive study be made for greater empathy with the animal itself.

AMERICAN GREEN TREE FROG

This species of frog is very common in the wild as well as a domestic pet. Favouring warm humid climates, it uses small sticky disks on the end of each toe with which to cling to leaves and branches.

KANGAROO

The kangaroo is native to Australia and lives in open country, moving in a series of bounds on strong hindlegs, whilst it's long, thick tail helps with balance and weight distribution.

ELEPHANT

Elephants grow taller and larger throughout their lives. Their travelling range once extended throughout most of the African Savanna, south of the Sahara. By flapping their large ears back and forth, elephants can significantly cool themselves by up to five degrees in the hot climate.

BLACK RHINOCEROS

The black rhino has a pointed upper lip, which is used to pluck leaves and twigs from trees and bushes. They are solitary animals, rarely congregating. The rhinoceros group emerged about 60 million years ago and today lives in southern Africa.

AMERICAN BISON

The American bison is a close relative to the European bison. The bison is a shaggy beast weighing 1 tonne (2,000 pounds). The Plains Indians relied greatly on the bison, or buffalo as they became known, principally as a source of food, but also within their mythology.

POLAR BEAR

The polar bear is the biggest and strongest predator of the Arctic . Although the polar bear is a very large 700 kilogram and three metre long animal it is surprisingly agile. The heavy coat and thick layer of blubber assists in keeping it warm when swimming in near-freezing water.

Drawing Animals

KOALA

The koala is a bear-like tree-dwelling marsupial from Australia, potentially vulnerable to extinction. Koalas feed predominantly on a restricted range of eucalyptus leaves, preferring an open forest and woodland habitat. Similar to the kangaroo, the koala raises its young in a pouch.

HARP SEAL

The Harp Seal has beautiful, lustrous dark eyes and is shy in demeanour. Young seals have a dense coat of fluffy white fur, which protects them from the cold and camouflages them against the white ice and any predators.

COMMON RINGTAIL POSSUM

The ringtail possum is a nocturnal creature, with a feature being the young born prematurly and developing inside their mother's pouch. Their long tail assists in anchoring them to tree branches when climbing to treetops and eating leaves and blossoms. The ringtail is a medium sized possum, weighing from 650 grams to 1000 grams.

DEER

Fallow deer are almost extinct in their original range in southern Europe and only survive in scattered populations. In summer, fallow deer have a light fawn coat with white spots and in winter, their coat turns greyer without spots, enabling camouflage the year round.

CHIMPANZEE

The chimp is an African ape and the third largest after the gorilla and the orangutan. Chimp's are also the best tool-users after men, using sticks and stones as tools and weapons. They are splendid climbers and quite acrobatic in the way they swing from branches and vines.

JAGUAR

The jaguar is the most powerful of the big cats indigenous to the Americas and looks like a heavier, short-legged leopard. Requiring large areas in which to hunt for its prey, it is however being increasingly driven into smaller environments. Though they climb trees, adult jaguars are not agile, weighing up to 110 kilograms and growing to 2.4 metres in length.

HIPPOPOTAMUS

Hippos generally live in rivers and head for water when frightened. Hippos spend their day in the water, choosing to come ashore to feed at night. Sleeping and resting in the water during the day, however if disturbed, they swiftly move to deeper water or reed beds, in which event, only their eyes and nostrils remain above

LIONESS

Lions live in groups, or 'prides', consisting of up to thirty individuals. At about three years of age, females become permanent members of the pride and begin to breed at about 4 years having 3 or 4 cubs at one time.

GIRAFFE

The giraffe is a tree-eater from Africa. With its long neck the giraffe can stretch for tender leaves up to 5.5 metres from ground level. Giraffes are timid and inoffensive towards other animals and live in loose social groups. The male giraffe is the tallest land animal and towers up to 5.4 metres in height, with females reaching 4.5 metres.

BEAVER

The beaver is the largest rodent in the northern hemisphere. Essentially an aquatic animal with webbed hindfeet serving as paddles and a broad flat tail utilised as a rudder.

GORILLA

Generally the gorilla is a quiet, sociable plant-eater. Despite its size, dominant posture and chest beating display, it rarely attacks. They are the largest and heaviest living primates. A mature male weighs up to 200 kilograms with a height of up to 1.8 metres tall. Gorillas spend 90 percent of their time on the ground as their size and weight makes them unsuited to tree life.

WOLF

Man has driven the wolf back to Europe, but it still lives as far south as Italy and Spain. This creature does not hibernate and only rarely stores food caches. Not all members of the pack reproduce at once, so responsibility for the cubs upbringing is shared between the entire group.

SEA OTTER

The smallest ocean mammal is the sea otter, a member of the weasel family. Males grow to 1.5 metres in length and weigh up to 40 kilograms. Sea otters fur insulates and protects them from polar waters through the warm jacket of air trapped between the layers of a dense coat.

RABBIT

The rabbit is a very adaptable animal, still widespread in northern Europe it has been severely culled elsewhere. Males are called bucks; females, does.